What Was It Like?™
BENJAMIN FRANKLIN

by Lawrence Weinberg
illustrated by Alex Bloch

Longmeadow Press

Published by Longmeadow Press
201 High Ridge Road, Stamford, CT 06904

ANGEL
ENTERTAINMENT INC.

Hello, my young friend. I'm Ben Franklin—and I'm glad to see that you're reading a book! All of my life I thought that reading was wonderful. I suppose that had a lot to do with a book my father had in our house called *Plutarch's Lives*. It was all about famous people who'd lived in the days of ancient Greece and Rome.

I don't remember who helped me to learn how to read it, or whether I taught myself. But there I was, a chunky little boy with that book in my lap, plowing through one big word after another...like a tiny ship bouncing over the waves.

What an adventure! I read those stories by sunlight and by the light of the candles my father made in his chandler shop in Boston town.

We Franklins lived behind and above that shop in the same house—seventeen children, although some of them had already grown up and moved away by the time I was born. That was on January 17, 1706. My father carried me through the snow to the church and named me after his older brother who lived in England. He told my mother that I was going to grow up to become a minister someday, just like our preacher, Reverend Cotton Mather.

My father thought a lot of Reverend Mather, even though the minister had supported the burn-

ing of a number of women for being witches about fourteen years earlier. Witchcraft was not the only thing Reverend Mather felt strongly about, however. He spent all his life preaching and writing sermons about how important it was to always *do good!*

Now, I believed in that, too. But believing it and *doing* it weren't always the same thing. There was one time when my friends and I went down to the marshes near the ocean. We liked to fish there, but at low tide you had to wade far out into the water to get at the fish we were after. I noticed that there was a big pile of stones on the shore. Some workmen had left the stones there. They were going to use them to build a house.

We hid until the workmen were gone. Then we picked up the heavy stones and carried them to the water. It was some job, laying them end to end! We worked for hours. But finally we had a stone path that took us right out to where the fish were!

I was very proud of what I'd done...until my father found out. I just couldn't understand why he insisted that we tear our jetty down.

"But everyone who wants to can fish from it," I pleaded. "Just come and look and you'll see how good it is!"

"Was it right," he asked me, "to take other people's property without their permission?"

"Well, no...."

"Then if something isn't right how can it ever be good?"

You can see that my father had a lot of good sense. Our neighbors knew it. Even though he only made soap and candles for a living, there were always folks coming to our house to ask his advice about all sorts of things.

Some of those people would stay for dinner—which was a treat for us. The food we Franklins had to eat was the same day after day. It was mostly milk with bread, or cornmeal mush in the morning, and a meat stew and a pudding for supper. But it was easy to forget about plain food when there were good times and wonderful conversations around the table!

We kids heard a lot of stories from these dinner guests about Indian raids and runaway slaves, and about pirates and battles on the sea between the English and the French.

The more I listened to these stories—and the more I went down to Boston harbor, where the sailing ships were—the more I wanted to go off to sea as a cabin boy, as had my oldest brother Josiah.

You see, the harbor was the most important thing about Boston. There were ships that went out after the great sperm whales, and ships that carried timber and clothing and sugar and tea and rum. There were ships that had been to England and Africa and the West Indies. Some had gone all the way down to the bottom of South America, sailed around the tip to the Pacific Ocean, and even on to China!

Many of the sailors had grown up in New England—just like my friends and I. Some were savages who wore necklaces of sharks' teeth around their throats, and had rings in their ears! Others were from all over the world.

How I longed to be off with them. But my father had different ideas for me. He did not want me to run away someday as my brother Josiah had done. Josiah had come home only once, after nine whole years, and then disappeared forever. No, I was going to become a minister. And to do that I would have to go to school. It would not be easy to send me. There were no free public schools then, and very few parents could afford the private ones. Only rich people sent their sons. And hardly anyone thought about sending their daughters.

I was eight when my father put me in a grammar school. But he pulled me out again when I was only ten! It wasn't because I hadn't done well. I'd been the best student in my class. Well, except for arithmetic, which I'll have to admit that I flunked.

My father had been noticing things about ministers. Not all of them were living in as nice a house as Reverend Mather. And many of them had more holes in their shoes and patches in their clothing than any candlemaker! Why spend all that money, my father thought, when he could teach me his own trade for free?

So I went to help him in the shop, cutting wicks and pouring tallow into the candle molds. Though I loved being with my father, I have to say that I hated every minute of working there. There was a huge vat of tallow that I sometimes had to stir. Before I was born, a brother of mine had fallen into that vat when he was only sixteen months old, and had drowned in the suds!

While *that* was working on my imagination, there was something else working on my nose. Tallow comes from boiling down the fat of animals. Oh, how I hated the stink of that greasy stuff! The smell followed me right out of the shop, clinging to my hair and clothes until I ran down to the ocean where the wind could blow it away!

I put up with two years of candlemaking. Mean-

while, my father was getting more and more worried that he'd wake up one morning and find that I had run off to sea.

The dear, good man couldn't bear that thought. He loved all of his family. And, sometimes, I even think he had a special place in his heart for me.

"I'm going to find a trade," he told my mother, "that Benjamin will like well enough to keep him here in Boston!"

He took me all around Boston to watch the carpenters building houses and the joiners fitting ships together and the blacksmiths working with metals. He showed me what their tools were like, and helped me practice using them, for he was wonderful at working with his hands.

What I learned then was very useful later on in life when I was fixing things and making models of my inventions. But we still hadn't found the right kind of work for a twelve-year-old boy with a love of adventure. Then my father hit upon it! He'd send me to work for my half-brother, James, who had opened a print shop.

In those days, a printer was an important person. If he didn't write books and pamphlets, he at least printed them. And my father knew that my love of the sea was almost as great as my love of books! I was excited by my father's idea.

There was only one little hitch. I had to sign a contract with my brother. It said that he would teach me the trade as his apprentice, but that I'd have to stay with him until I was twenty-one! That was nine whole years! For the first eight of them I wouldn't get any money at all, just food and a place to sleep.

My father saw that there were going to be problems because brothers, you know, are sometimes likely to quarrel. He said I could talk to him if things got difficult. So I signed the contract and moved into a boarding house with James and his other apprentices.

To tell you the truth, I was pretty happy the first two or three years. Printers' ink was one smell I didn't mind. And it was all right with me to run errands and do a lot of floor sweeping. Just as long as I also got to put together the metal letters that we called "type" until they spelled out words, and dip the type in the ink, and work the handle of the big press when it printed everything out on paper!

One of the best parts about working at the print shop was getting to meet people who sold books for a living. I'd borrow a book overnight and read it by candlelight. First thing in the morning I'd give it back, good as new and ready to be sold.

There were some books, though, that I wanted

to buy—but James wasn't giving me any money. One day I approached him with the kind of business offer that a Franklin would listen to. "How would you like to save half the money you spend on me for food?" I asked.

That made his ears perk up like a horse's. "How?"

"Just give me half, and let me buy my own meals!"

"Done!" he said.

Well, I wasn't eating meat in those days, so I saved money right there. Often I just got along with a glass of water, a slice of bread and some raisins. And though now and then I treated myself to a little pastry from the bakery shop, this left me a few coins for buying books. As soon as I was finished, I would trade those for more books. (By the way, I used one of them to finally teach myself arithmetic.)

But it seemed as though the more I learned, the harder it became for me to get along with my brother. James would get angry at me for speaking up and making suggestions. When he thought I was talking back to him or showing off how smart I was, he'd beat me.

I was very strong for my age, but he was a lot stronger. Besides, I was his apprentice. I couldn't do anything when he hit me except think about how unfair it was. I felt that my brother was taking advantage of his power over me. And nobody, not even a king, should do that! I really wanted to leave him. Yet what could I do? I'd signed that contract.

Then things became very interesting around the print shop. My brother decided to start a newspaper, *The New England Courant.* It was the third one in Boston—and the only one that wasn't boring. He and his friends who wrote for it poked fun at everybody, from the governor to old Cotton Mather—the minister who had written all those sermons telling us to *do good.*

When I asked James to let me write for the *Courant,* he told me to forget about it because I was only sixteen. But I didn't. I just wrote a letter to the editor in different handwriting and pretended to be a poor but well-bred young woman in her twenties. I signed it, *"Your Humble Servant, Silence Dogood."*

And guess what? James thought it was so good that he printed it! The readers of the *Courant* liked it. They wanted more. So, once a week after that...in the dead of night...I would slip another letter under the print shop door.

Now, Silence was a thoughtful young woman

who didn't often get angry. But one of her letters talked about all of the men who were against having their own sisters and daughters get an education.

"How can you say that women are too silly to talk about important things," she wanted to know, "when you men in your wisdom don't want them to learn about important things?"

People laughed a lot when they read those letters. Their laughter made it easier for them to think about things that otherwise might have upset them too much. I hoped that my brother would do some laughing and thinking, too, when I finally told him who Mistress Dogood really was.

It didn't turn out that way. James felt tricked. He became jealous when his own grown-up friends began to treat me like one of them. The quarrels got worse. And so did the beatings.

Finally I decided that no contract ever gave one person the right to abuse another. I waited for the right time to run away. And then came the day when a group of chiefs from the Eight Indian Nations of the East and their families arrived to visit Boston—and to watch how our government worked. The whole town turned out to welcome them, and to see John Quittamog, the one hundred-twelve-year-old Mohawk.

This was my chance. Quickly, I slipped through the streets and jumped aboard a ship, paid for my passage, and sailed away! I had almost nothing left in my pockets. I was seventeen years old.

We had fair winds behind our sails as we headed south along the coast. "Now I'm free!" I thought. "At last I can follow the sea!" But something in me seemed to be shaking its head, reminding me how hard I'd already worked to become a printer.

"Yes," I cried, "but I want adventure!"

"Why?" asked that other voice inside of me. "Can't a printer's life be an adventure also?" Three days later, when we docked in New York, I went looking for a job. It was not a very big town then, although it was much fancier than Boston and people even ate with something they called a fork. There was only one printer, and he didn't have enough business to hire an assistant.

"But if you're willing to go on to Philadelphia," he said, "you might find work there."

First I took an old ferryboat to cross to the Jersey Shore. The boat should have made it in no time, but a storm blew up that tore off her sails. Everyone aboard got soaked to the skin. We were tossed around for thirty hours before we landed. After that I still had fifty miles of walking ahead of me—and it poured rain all the way for two days straight. I was tired and miserable and I squished water from every part of me, but at last I found a riverboat that was going the rest of the way. I helped with the rowing, and the next morning, there it was—Philadelphia!

I got out on the dock looking like something even a cat would have thrown back. But I was happy—and starving! Someone showed me where the nearest bakery was. I went in and plunked down almost all of my money—three pennies! I didn't know whether food was cheap in Philadelphia or the baker took pity on me. He gave me three of the longest buns I had ever seen.

So up the street I went, one bun tucked under each arm and another one jammed into my mouth, when a pretty girl saw me. She was standing in her doorway, and didn't know that someday I was going to marry her! She took one look at all the rolls, and another at the extra clothes I had poking out of my pockets, and decided I was the silliest sight she had ever seen!

I saw some pretty strange-looking people, myself. They were wearing very wide hats and the plainest clothes in the world. I later found out that they were called Quakers. They were all walking towards a building. Since it was Sunday, I thought it must be a church. I followed them inside, sat down in one of the pews—and fell fast asleep. I don't know if I snored. Philadelphia was called the City of Brotherly Love, and of all the people in it, the Quakers were the kindest. No one woke me until the prayer meeting was over, and then someone helped me find a place to stay.

The next day, I cleaned myself up as best I could, then went to see a printer named Keimer. He had just opened his shop and had bought himself a broken printing press that he didn't know how to fix. After I put it into working order for him, I found out that he didn't know all that much about using it, either. So he hired me to do his printing jobs.

This Mr. Keimer was partly honest, partly a crook, and partly crazy. He never bothered to learn to do anything for himself, and yet he believed that he was a great man. One day he told me that he wanted to start a new religion, with himself as the leader of it. Since I was pretty good with ideas, he told me I would have to make up all the rules!

Now that I'm older, I don't think it was such a nice joke that I played on him. But I just couldn't help saying, "All right. My first rule is, that as the head of our new religion, you have to set a good example and give up eating meat forever."

I knew very well that meat was just about the only food that that poor man ever *did* eat! For days and weeks he tried to stay away from it—but in his dreams he kept being haunted by plates of ham and pork. Finally, he couldn't take it any longer and gulped down an entire roast pig!

That was the end of his new religion, but not of his desire to be considered important. Which is why he was so excited when, one day, who should walk into the shop but his Excellency, the governor of the Colony of Pennsylvania.

But Governor Keith asked for me! "My dear Master Benjamin," he said, making a sweeping bow. "A relative of yours has shown me a letter you wrote to him about why you left Boston, and I must say that you explain yourself very well, for being such a young man. I thought it might be very amusing to have a good meal with you. Won't you join me for a spot of lunch?"

After that, the governor and I saw a lot of each other. We talked about books and ideas and told each other funny stories. He thought I was a fine fellow and a very hard worker, too. So, one day, he made me an offer.

"Get your father to lend you the money to open a print shop of your own," he said, "and I will help you find all the business you need."

Of course I went straight back to Boston. My parents were so happy to see me! They were proud, too, at how well I had done in only a few months. But when my father read the letter the governor had written to him, he shook his head.

"There's something I don't trust about this man," he said. "It seems to me that he praises an eighteen-year-old boy too much. You don't know enough yet about what people are like, Benjamin, to be running a business. Come back when you are twenty-one and then I'll help you."

I was disappointed, of course. But when I got back to Philadelphia, the governor thumped his fist on the table. "Never mind! You just go to England to buy the printing press and everything else you need for your print shop. I will give you a letter to the sellers, instructing them to send all the bills to me. What do you say?"

I didn't have to be asked twice. I bought a ticket with my own money. Then I went to the governor's house to ask for the letter he'd promised me.

"The governor is too busy to see you," I was told. "But don't worry. The governor will send the letter down to the ship and the captain will hold it for you."

When I went aboard ship a few days later, I saw a whole bagful of letters being delivered to the captain, so I thought no more about it. I was too excited, I suppose, about my first voyage overseas.

We hoisted sail—and off we went. What a rough crossing that turned out to be! It was wintertime, when the North Atlantic can be at its worst. Storm after storm blew up. For weeks we rolled and rocked and got driven off course. What an adventure! When we arrived in England on Christmas Eve, I was as excited as a young horse being let out of the stable.

But first I had to get that letter the captain was supposed to be holding for me.

"I am most sorry, Mr. Franklin," said the captain. "But the governor did not send any letter for you."

"You must be mistaken," I insisted. "See there. That's a letter from the governor. I recognize his handwriting."

The captain let me open the envelope. The letter had nothing to do with money. And nothing to do with me. It was for somebody else!

There was a passenger on board who knew the governor far better than I did. "That fellow," he said, "makes a lot of promises because he wants everyone to like him. But then he never keeps his promises!"

Now I was thousands of miles from home, and as poor as I had been when I first went to Philadelphia. But so what? London had the best printing houses in the world.

Right away I got a job and set to work. The hours were long, but I didn't mind. While I was putting the books on the presses I was also reading what was in them! In those days everyone was just becoming excited about science, which was very new. I could learn about the latest discov-

eries and experiments. I could also read about all sorts of new ideas on religion and government and, well, you name it.

The English printers with whom I worked were interesting people. No one believed more than they did in the free exchange of ideas. Yes, I learned a great deal in the year-and-a-half that I was in that country. On the voyage back I had plenty of time to think about the kind of person that I wanted to become.

That person, I decided, would be honest and fair with everyone. He'd be careful not to show off, or make others feel foolish. This Benjamin would be truthful with himself about his own faults and try to mend them. Most of all, he would try to help the world become a better place.

Back in Philadelphia, one of the first things I did was put together a club of young people like myself who wanted to read books and discuss ideas. We called our club the Junto, although some people nicknamed it the "Leather Apron Club," because most of our members were craftsmen who wore leather aprons when they worked. Later on I thought it would be a good idea if we brought all our books together and kept them where we met. That way we could borrow them from each other whenever we wanted.

This was the start of the first lending library anywhere in America. When news of our group spread, other people began setting up libraries. After a while there were lending libraries all over the Colonies. More and more folks were now able to spend time reading since they didn't have to send all the way across the ocean for books.

My friends and I tried to do whatever we could to make Pennsylvania a better and safer place, so we organized the first fire department. We were also just getting started in our careers, so we made a solemn promise to help each other. A couple of my fellow members lent me the money to buy my own print shop. And the others sent me customers!

Now that I had a printing press of my own, I decided to do a little writing myself. I wrote a little booklet to convince people that it was time to have paper money in the Colonies because there weren't enough coins to go around. Soon a law was passed in the Pennsylvania colonial legislature to print paper money.

Guess who got the job of printing it?

Now that I could afford it, I decided to get married. I really loved Deborah Read, that girl who had laughed at me on my first day in Philadelphia. Being my father's practical son, I also thought that a wife would be a very good help around the house and in the shop. I needed that help, since I was now beginning to spend time working on my new ideas—like publishing an almanac.

I wasn't so sure of Debbie's feelings. I hadn't written to her much while I was in England, so she had married someone else. Now her husband was dead, but was she still angry with me?

Well, you don't get anywhere if you don't ask, so I asked. She said yes!

Now that *that* was settled, I could begin to work on my almanac. Almanacs were just about the only books many people read besides the Bible. They gave farmers advice about when it would be best to plant their crops. They tried to predict all of the next year's weather and the ocean tides. They told seafarers when it would be safe to start a long voyage. They gave remedies for colds, described what your next child might be like and gave many other kinds of advice.

Unfortunately, crops still failed and ships still sank and children still turned out to be what you didn't expect—because most of the predictions came from reading the stars.

I thought I could write a more helpful almanac than the one that was already being published in Philadelphia by a man named Titan Leeds. I also thought that I'd have some fun. Making believe that my name was Richard, I sent out an announcement. It said that I had just read the stars and learned a terrible fact. Mr. Leeds would not be publishing next year's almanac...because he was going to drop dead! And since I was a poor man whose wife insisted that he make some money, I had decided to try writing an almanac of my own.

Mr. Titan Leeds did not think very highly of my little prediction. In fact, he raised a terrible fuss—for which I was very thankful. It got everybody's attention, and then they all went out to buy my book! When they read *Poor Richard's Almanac*, folks found a lot more jokes inside. But they also found sayings from very wise people who had lived in other times and other lands. There were

ideas, too, that my friends had talked about in our club, the Junto. Especially ideas about freedom. And each year I added facts about the latest scientific discoveries.

Yes, I was thinking about science more and more, and about how it could help people. In those days, you know, the only way to heat a house was to build a fire. But most of the heat from the burning logs would go straight up the chimney. In winter, people would have to stand very close to the fireplace to keep warm, or else bury themselves under lots of clothes and blankets. Now, new ideas had come along about heat, and I found a way to use them. I made a stove that could fit right inside the fireplace and send almost all the heat back into the room! When folks asked me why I wouldn't take any money for this invention, I just said, "Nobody ever charged *me* for those ideas!"

But the newest thing that everybody was excited about was electricity. There were performers who went around the countryside giving other people little shocks and making their hair stand on end. I have to admit that I was one of them, though I always warned folks first, of course.

One day, while I was making sparks fly in little glass bottles that were called Leyden jars, I noticed something. Those tiny electric sparks looked exactly like lightning flashes in the sky. For thousands of years folks had thought that lightning was God's way of showing His power and, sometimes, His anger. They thought these crackling bolts of light were like earthquakes in the sky.

I thought I'd try an experiment. On a rainy day, my son William and I went out to fly a kite. It was made of silk, but it was attached to a metal wire to attract electricity.

The kite went up, up, up—until it soared high overhead. After a while, tiny strands began sticking up on the string that held the kite. They looked like little hairs standing up on a person's head. I had tied a metal key near the bottom of the string, and now I touched it with my knuckle.

Well, I was very lucky that day because I could have been killed by the shock. The bolt shook me from head to toe. But I had proved it. Lightning was electricity!

Now, how was I going to use this knowledge to help people? I thought about all the wooden houses that had been struck by lightning and had burned to the ground—sometimes with the people who lived there still inside them—and it came to me. Lightning rods! Let each house have a metal

rod sticking up above the rooftop, I thought. The rod would attract the lightning before it reached the house. If the bottom of the rod were in the ground, a lightning bolt would travel through it and leave the house alone! The house would be saved!

Poor Richard's Almanac for the year 1753 told everyone exactly how to make and use a lightning rod. You have no idea how excited people got. The news traveled all around the world. People started to call me Dr. Franklin, even though I had never graduated from a school. I became very famous.

In those days, an educated person wanted to be good at a lot of different things. A poet might also become a politician. A soldier might try his hand at designing buildings. And a printer who had turned scientist in his spare time could also be hired by the King of England to do something about improving the postal system among the Colonies. I became His Majesty's American Post-master General!

To do this, I had to travel all over the Thirteen Colonies. As I did, I began to see that we really needed to be one big united country! I thought very hard about this. When I later traveled to

England, I tried to explain my ideas to anyone who would listen.

I found some people who felt very friendly towards their "American cousins," as we were sometimes called. They gave my ideas a lot of thought. But the men who ran the country simply shook their heads.

Americans, they said, didn't need to be united. As a matter of fact, they thought we shouldn't even be trying to make laws for ourselves in the separate Colonies! They believed England had the sole right to make all the important laws for its possessions.

"Fine," I said. "No problem. Just let us elect representatives to be in *your* government in England. That way we can all work *together* to make the laws."

"Oh, no!" they replied. "Our government is only for Englishmen!"

"But how can we be loyal to you," I asked, in as calm a voice as I could, "if you won't treat us the way you treat yourselves?"

It was no use. They just wouldn't listen. But I kept at it. There were other things I asked them for, too. I wanted them to help the Indian tribes who had been cheated out of land on the western frontier. "This will stop the terrible raids by the tribes against the settlers," I said. But again they ignored me.

Pennsylvania's elected assembly had asked me to be a representative. They desperately needed permission to raise money at home through taxes. This way they could help the Colony to build and grow.

"Yes, we will think about it," was all the Englishmen ever told me, covering their mouths so I wouldn't see them yawn.

I could understand why they were getting bored with me. I was bored myself. I'd spent five years in England, asking over and over for the same things. Then I went home, took a deep breath, and came back again to spend ten years more!

But the treatment of the Colonies only got worse—and I had to ask myself why. It was from England, really, that we Americans had learned all about elections and other freedoms. Why did they treat us so?

Then I thought of my older brother, James, and about how he had treated me in the print shop—calling me a smart aleck and complaining to my father that I was talking back to him. Each time I'd had a good idea he'd grown angrier, until finally he'd started to beat me up. I wondered if countries could get the same way about their own "younger brothers." I wondered if they could get jealous and frightened, too.

Thoughts like these could make even a jolly man sad. And to add to it, my sweet wife had died while I was away. I had grown old trying to keep the quarrel between America and England from getting worse. All it ever needed, I thought, was just a little common sense. Too much time had passed without using it.

Now I wanted independence with all my heart. It was the only way, I decided, that we Americans could stand up for ourselves and run our own lives. I had hoped we could win independence someday without war, but things were moving too fast now. There was trouble brewing in the Colonies. Revolutionary committees were springing up everywhere—especially in Massachusetts. Many British people actually blamed *me* for this, so I sailed for America before someone decided to throw me in jail.

By the time I arrived home, the Revolution had already started! "Well, if it's here, it's here," I thought. "There's nothing to do now but win it!"

The leaders of the rebellion held a meeting in Philadelphia. And young Thomas Jefferson—with just a little fatherly advice from me—wrote the Declaration of Independence. When we signed

it on July 4, 1776, I made a joke that was really quite serious, "We must, indeed, all hang together, or most assuredly we shall all hang separately."

George Washington of Virginia was made commander in chief. But where would he get the money to pay for his army? "From England's biggest enemy!" said the leaders of the Continental Congress. They asked me to go to France to plead for help from King Louis the Sixteenth.

I was seventy years old, and suffering from an illness that often made it hard for me to stand. I had lost my wife, and my son William had broken my heart by siding with the British. Still, how could I refuse to take on the job? I was the only American about whom many French people had heard. They'd read *Poor Richard*, and used my lightning rods. I already knew many fine French people who had thought deeply about liberty.

My two wonderful grandsons agreed to go with

me to France. We packed up a small printing press, and a bathtub I had made for myself. It had a lid that closed over the top, so I could soak for as long as I wanted while visitors sat and talked to me. We sailed on the good ship *Reprisal,* which was fast enough to get away from the English ships that were on the lookout to capture me. The people in France welcomed me as if I were a hero. People cried and the young ladies fondly called me "Papa!"

But when I went to meet the king, I found I had a terrible problem. For some reason, my wig didn't fit me right. What good were my fancy clothes if I couldn't use my wig? Why, without a wig in those days you looked like a farmer, or a fisherman...or a printer.

"And what on earth, Ben Franklin," I asked myself, "is so wrong with *that*?"

A gasp was heard throughout the palace when the elegant gentlemen and ladies saw me walking

bareheaded through the most elegant court in all the world.

"What a scandal!" they whispered to each other. But the king only smiled. He took me by the hand, like one ordinary man to another, and said just as simply as I was dressed, "Please tell America of my friendship."

The French did help us a great deal after that meeting, though they couldn't always give us everything we wanted. Every war is too long, and this one dragged on for seven whole years.

"There never was a good war, nor a bad peace," I said when we'd won our freedom at last. Then I sailed for home—the new America.

I won't tell you whether I cried a tear or two as the long voyage ended. But perhaps I did take off those bifocal glasses I had invented, to give them a little wipe, as our ship drew nearer to the city. The people of Philadelphia were waiting for me on the docks when I arrived, and the bells of the city were ringing.

Later, in the quiet hours, I asked myself, "What now, Ben Franklin? Ready to die yet?"

"Not yet," I answered myself. "There is something that is deeply troubling me."

I was thinking about the slaves. Once I'd even had slaves of my own. But now I became president of a society for the abolition of slavery. With the last of my strength, I wrote a pamphlet calling for an end to the most terrible injustice there could ever be in the Land of Freedom.

On a quiet night in 1790, I looked back upon my life. It had been wonderful, but now I was tired. I looked ahead and wondered about the future of our beloved country. There was still so much to be done to keep the Liberty Bell ringing out forever, so that we would all be free and we would all be equal!

There was a rope tied to that bell. If people stopped tugging on it, the bell's great song would cease. Now I had to let go of that rope, as so many of my friends had already done. Who would come after us to help pull it?

I certainly hope that *you* will, my young friend. It seems to me that your hands are perfect for the job. They are already holding a book.

Sayings from
Poor Richard's Almanac

Eat to live, not live to eat.
Half-wits talk much, but say little.
He that cannot obey, cannot command.
Be slow in choosing a friend, slower in
changing one.
Well done is better than well said.
God helps them that help themselves.
It's better to take many injuries than to give one.
Being ignorant is not so much shame as being
unwilling to learn.
If your head is wax, don't walk in the sun.
He that lies down with dogs shall rise up
with fleas.
A good example is the best sermon.
When a well's dry, we know the worth of water.

The Life and Times of
Benjamin Franklin

1706   On January 17, Ben Franklin is born in Boston, Massachusetts.

1721   Ben's brother, James, starts *The New England Courant*, one of the first newspapers in the British Colonies.

1723   In October, Ben goes to Philadelphia.

1724   In December, Ben arrives almost penniless in England.

1726   Ben returns to Philadelphia.

1730   Ben opens his own print shop in Philadelphia, and marries Deborah Read.

1731   Ben starts the first circulating library in the Colonies in the city of Philadelphia.

1732   First issue of *Poor Richard's Almanac* is published.

1736   Ben organizes the first fire department in Philadelphia—a very good idea since almost all of the buildings are made of wood.

1752   Ben proves through electrical experiments with a kite that lightning is electricity.

1753   Ben becomes Postmaster General of the Colonies.

1754   The French and Indian War begins and lasts until 1763.

1757   Ben goes to London as the representative from the Colony of Pennsylvania.

1762   Ben returns to America from England.

1764   Ben goes to England again and stays until 1775. On his way home, the American Revolution breaks out at the battles of Concord and Lexington.

1765   The Stamp Act is passed. This gives the British Parliament the right to tax the Colonies without giving them any representation in government. It is repealed in 1766 largely because of Ben's efforts.

1776   First Continental Congress is held in Philadelphia. Ben is a delegate. On July 4, the Declaration of Independence is officially announced, and America is born.

1777   An English army is defeated in Saratoga, New York, by American soldiers. This victory enables Ben to persuade France to join America in the fight against the British.

1781   In October, British General Cornwallis surrenders to George Washington at Yorktown, Virginia. America has won the war!

1783   On September 3, the official signing of the peace treaty between England and America takes place at the Palace of Versailles in France.

1785   Ben returns home to a hero's welcome.

1787   In May, Ben is the oldest delegate (at the age of eighty-one) at the First Constitutional Convention. The Constitution is signed in September.

1790   On April 17, Ben dies at the age of eighty-four.